1

THE JOURNEY OF JUNIOR GARCIA

INTRODUCTION

In September of 2012, while catching up on my current events reading by scanning months' old headlines, I came across this story and I was compelled to learn more:

On July 13, 2012, a nineteen-year-old college student named Junior Garcia, completed a walking pilgrimage from his home in Fort Worth, Texas to Washington, D.C.

Few teens (or adults, for that matter), would give up their summer to walk on blistered feet for nearly 1300 miles to demonstrate their faith. Let's be honest. It's difficult to get some of us to spend an hour doing anything other than "preferred activities" during our time off from work or school. Junior spent thirty-seven days in the middle of the summer walking along the country's interstates in scorching heat for his faith. While walking, step by step, he carried a wooden cross on his back and over his shoulders.

According to Junior, he did it to show the love of Christ for all of humanity.

Although Junior didn't know it at the time, he was not the first person to take the scripture found in Matthew 16:24 literally. In Matthew 16:24, Jesus instructs his disciples by saying, "If any man will come after me, let him deny himself, and take up his cross, and follow me." Arthur Blessit, a traveling preacher who in the 60's focused on talking to kids about Christ in Hollywood, is credited with carrying the cross through every nation of the world. What was accomplished by God through the lifelong ministry of Mr. Blessit is not to be taken lightly. However, in a time when some teens will literally take a life before being embarrassed, looking weak or foolish, a quiet and introverted Junior Garcia put himself out there to be ridiculed, criticized, and laughed at.

A month after reading the story and contacting his pastor, I flew to Texas to meet with Junior, his family, church, and anyone connected with this story. When I was first introduced in person to Junior, I quickly realized that he possessed an authentic humility and was extremely down to earth. Some would say he was just "raised right." While it is true that he was reared in a godly household, I thought, *So are many other teens.* Yet, they chose not to demonstrate their faith publicly.

As a teen, I was so involved in feeding every fleshly desire I possessed, that there was no way I would have made a sacrifice for anyone other than myself. I lived a self-serving lifestyle and was blindly unaware of the harm I could do to myself, others, or my future. During that period in my life, *me* time was all the time. Demonstrating my faith was the furthest idea from my mind. And here was Junior Garcia, a quiet nineteen-year old, putting himself out there to share his faith with the world without denouncing the faith of others.

The more I interviewed Junior and his family, the more curious I became. Despite the negativity frequently being reported on the daily news, I am always excited and encouraged by the leaps toward excellence I have experienced with members

4

of the Millennial and Generation Z groups. Their hunger for authenticity is both inspiring and uplifting.

But there was more to Junior's story than basic inspiration. His expression of faith moved people in such a way that they had to re-examine their own spiritual lives and, in doing so, take action. Junior's story forcefully continued to push open the floodgates of my mind with questions: *Who really inspired him to make this journey? How could he prove that it was God stirring his spirit and not his own ego? Could he have misinterpreted what God was saying to him? How did he convince his family to join him? Why did he choose to pursue God now in his life? How did he succeed in inspiring people of all ages to discover ways in which they could demonstrate their faith in Christ?*

As a youth, I regularly attended church and claimed to be a Christian, but I had not committed to living for anyone except for myself. Heck, despite being taught in church school that God could use anyone, I rarely considered being used by God. If that ever was to happen, it would have to happen when I was much older. In fact, at that time, I thought of my life as my own, and I wanted to live it my way.

Junior, on the other hand, had positively inspired people in such a way that they wanted more from their lives. More importantly, they wanted more from their spiritual lives. Wow! Now that's impact! Additionally, as we read the Bible, we find out that God uses young people throughout biblical history. Joseph, Daniel, David, Rebekah, and Miriam are just a few names of people whom God worked through to impact lives and, in some cases, the lives of an entire nation.

I continued to find myself reflecting, while comparing my own late teen years with those of Junior Garcia's. My path to discovering my role in God's kingdom began many years earlier on the inner-city streets of Newark, New Jersey. I made a conscious decision to live differently. I walked away from a lifestyle that I had previously idolized. Junior's path began when he responded to a call to demonstrate his Christian faith by attempting to walk nearly 1300 miles. Although there are decades between our ages, we are both serving with a single goal in mind: to share with you the reason behind such an extreme demonstration of faith.

While preparing Junior's story for a documentary, I identified ten biblical "action" principles that enabled a quiet kid from Texas to complete a long cross walk in July of 2012, but also to influence others to take their faith to another level and some to create their own ministries. God has given us these principles in his word. The principles form a single word that answer the question, "How did God use Junior's journey to make such an impact on others?" The word is *eternalize*.

Eternalize is a verb which means *to give eternal or lasting existence to.* From the verb, we form the acronym ETERNALIZE, which stands for:

E - **Embrace** your background

T - **Trust** God

E - **Engage** your era

R - **Renew** your mind

N - **Notice** God's voice

A - **Ask** God

L - **Learn** adversity's purpose

I - **Inspire** others

Z - **Zoom-in** on the cross

E - **Express** thanks

Special Note:

This book was not written to simply be a narrative. It was written to illuminate the biblical principles that were employed before and after one teen's amazing journey. Excerpts of the Journey story have been extracted to help illustrate how God equipped a nineteen-year-old for Christian service. For a more comprehensive story, told by those who participated in the Journey, view the documentary *The Journey of Junior Garcia.*

R. E. LeBlanc

Coastal Virginia

2017

One

ETERNALIZE

Embrace *your background*

"And we know that in all things God works for the good of those who love him, who have been called according to his purpose." (Romans 8:28, NIV)

~~~~~~

~~~~~~~~~~

The last months of Logan Price's junior year of high school was simply crazy and filled with excitement, anxiety and stress. After all, he began to realize that this phase of his life would quickly end. For Logan, however, it wasn't coming as quickly as he wanted it to. There were times when he wasn't sure if he would make it through to graduation.

His mother described his challenge: "He really struggled with math ever since he was in seventh grade, so we hired a tutor. It made a huge difference."

Following his junior year, Logan enlisted in the Split Training Option program for the Army National Guard. The program allowed him to complete basic training during the summer, go back to school to finish his senior year, and then return to the Army for Advanced Individual Training after his high school graduation.

Four-and-a-half years later, Logan enrolled in an alternative teaching certification program. Today, Mr. Price, as he is now called, is teaching math full-time at his alma mater. In his first year, he was recognized by his students, faculty, and staff as teacher of the year. When asked how he ended up back in high school, he replied, "Somehow along the way, I realized that I'd been preparing to do what I do now. My military training, background, and education gave me the tools I'd need for this career."

~ ~ ~

Similarly, Junior Garcia's background played a role in his completion of the Journey.

In 1992, Michelle Davis and her boyfriend, Jorge "BB" Garcia, were an average teenage couple. They spent a considerable amount of time together and appeared to be inseparable. The nickname "BB" had been coined by Michelle. When she heard Jorge's, mother call her son "Baby", it sounded more like BB. The name stuck. Later that year, during the summer, Michelle and BB would discover that they were about to become teenage parents.

On the day Michelle took the pregnancy test, she was home alone. "I took the test and when it showed up positive, I was scared to death," she remembered.

This was not the plan that she had for her life. In fact, she had recently received an offer to play volleyball for the University of North Texas. Michelle intended to study nursing. Suddenly, life became real—a little too real. She decided to wait a day or two before sharing the results of the pregnancy test with BB.

The moment arrived when she made known their dilemma. That day, as the teenage couple sat on the bed deciding what to do, Michelle had an idea. She grabbed two sheets of paper from a notebook. She handed one piece to BB and kept one for herself.

"We're gonna both write down yes or no if we should have the baby or not," Michelle announced.

"Okay," BB responded.

After both of them had written on their individually folded pieces of paper, Michelle opened each one to show BB. Written clearly on both papers was the word "yes."

At the time of this decision, Michelle lived in a Section 8 housing project and was on public assistance. BB's living arrangement was not ideal, either. He resided with his family in a two-bedroom home. The home had one bathroom and BB had five siblings. It was neither the right time nor circumstance for them to bring another life into the world.

Since Michelle was a child of divorced parents, she told her mother first about the pregnancy. Her mother responded without a single bit of condemnation and added a few hugs and tears. *That went surprisingly well*, the couple thought, but then they had to tell her father.

Michelle was more afraid and extremely nervous when telling her father than she had been with her mother. He was a man of few words, which added to the unpredictability of his response. With a youthful boldness, BB decided to be the one to inform Michelle's father. BB walked in to tell his future father-in-law that his daughter would give birth to a child, while Michelle remained outside the room.

After sharing the news, BB returned to Michelle along with her father. Her speechless but emotion-filled father gave her a passionate hug, and the couple drove off.

Once inside the car, Michelle asked, "What did he say?"

"I told him that you were pregnant," BB said. "Then he said 'Well, all I ask is that you take care of my daughter and that baby.'"

BB said that he assured the man, "I can promise you I'll do that."

BB did not expect the news to go over as well with his own parents. Instead, he imagined he'd hear a long lecture and the expression of tremendous disappointment. However, to BB's surprise, his parents gently encouraged him to go to college and continue to play sports.

The young couple lived with both Michelle's mother and BB's parents before they found a place of their own. Michelle refused to get married at the time, so they waited. She wanted to know that BB loved her and was not just interested in doing the right thing by marrying her.

Nine months after Junior was born, the two became husband and wife.

BB remembers meeting Michelle back in 1985. She had transferred into the Lake Worth school district from the Diamond Hill area during their sixth-grade year. They had mutual friends but didn't spend much time in conversation with each other, because BB was focused on his athletic life.

It wasn't until their freshmen year in high school that they began to take notice of one another. They were both on the school's track team. Since it was a small school, the male and female athletes would spend the entire day together during the track meets. Michelle and BB began to discover the compatibility within their respective personalities. BB respected Michelle's athletic prowess and determination. The couple was very different in demeanor, but they enjoyed each other's company. Although uninterested in girls, BB was popular amongst them, and they liked him.

BB had taken a leadership role on the track team and began to instruct Michelle on improving her performance. He clearly remembers what was attractive about Michelle at the time.

16

"Since I'm an athlete, I liked the way she played sports. She hustled and had a determination about her. She played the sport the way that I liked to see it played. There was an 'I'm gonna do whatever it takes to win' attitude," BB says.

What began as a mutually-admiring friendship between the two soon led to them spending time together during school hours as well. BB had a positive influence on Michelle from the beginning. During her sophomore year, she tried out for the cheerleading team. Previously uninterested in cheerleading, she desperately wanted to be a part of BB's football playing experience, which would maximize their time together. Michelle made the squad, which made the two inseparables as friends. That year, during track season, BB asked Michelle out. He wanted to make their romance official.

A couple of months later, while riding home on the bus from a track meet, BB made a proclamation to Michelle.

"Hey you," BB said, while grabbing Michelle's attention.

"What?"

"I don't like you anymore."

"Okay. . . are you serious?"

"You don't understand, I don't like you because. . . I love you."

This teenage declaration laid a foundation by which Michelle and BB would build a relationship that would sustain the challenges in the years to come.

BB remembers a lot of big decisions that came up quickly after Michelle became pregnant. More importantly, having the love and support of friends, school staff, and immediate family made all the difference during those early years. In fact, students, faculty and staff of their high school gave Michelle and BB a baby shower to help them out. In a separate incident, during school one day, BB's counselor called him into her office. Defending his decision to support his family, he adamantly told her that he was not going to college after high school. She chose not to put up a fight and took the liberty to arrange an interview for him with United Parcel Service.

~ ~ ~

When Junior accepted his call to demonstrate his faith, he knew that it wasn't impossible. He remembered how he had been the product of teen parents. He knew that there was nothing too hard for God because he had seen where his family members had started and how far they had come. God uses our background to prepare us for opportunities to serve him.

Junior's environment equipped him for the challenges he would one day face on the Journey. In the beginning of his story, the conditions and surroundings of which he was born didn't look too promising. His parents were seventeen-year-old seniors in high school. His grandparents on his mother's side were divorced. His father lived in a home that was too small for the size of their family. At the time, neither of his parents had a relationship with God. Most importantly, he was in danger of not being born at all. Michelle confessed, "Neither one of us was in church at the time. We weren't Christians. It even crossed my mind, *did I even want to have this baby?*"

But the Lord was building within Junior a heart that knew he could depend on and count on Him. Junior knew from his experiences and the experiences of his parents that if God started it, He'd complete it. How unlikely was it that God would bring about a teen who would serve Him and inspire others while expressing his love for his creator? It was highly likely for Junior, who believed that God could do it. Additionally, Junior's environment prepared him physically for the Journey. His parents were both high school athletes, which influenced the way Junior thought about diet, exercise, and physical activity. This attitude toward athletics obviously impacted Junior's behavior.

Some of us grow up in loving and supportive environments like the one in which Junior was reared. Eventually, his parents placed their faith in Christ and decided to live as Christians. They didn't have much in terms of material possessions in the beginning, but they had what they needed. And, most of all, they had support from their family and friends.

Nevertheless, some are born into a life of privilege. Their parents are well educated. They live in affluent neighborhoods. They attend the best schools. They fill the AP and Honors classrooms because they learn the value of a good education early and can afford it.

Others are brought up in environments where the poverty level and high school dropout rates are high. Instead of first learning how to read, many must learn to defend themselves. It can be toxic, violent, high-stressed, and too often drug-infested. Those who lack understanding even question whether God is present in these environments.

In America, the wealthiest and poorest communities are often a 5 to 20-mile drive away from each other or closer. I can't imagine God being smaller than a twenty-mile radius. My point is that God lives within His people. His people make up communities. There are elements, such as habits, patterns and attitudes in every environment that conflict with God's standards. As Christians, we'll need to leave behind some of the environmental elements that stunt our spiritual growth.

Nevertheless, wherever we were born or whoever we were born to, we need to believe that God knows what He is doing. He knew who our parents would be. He also knew which neighborhood, city, state, and country in which we would live. We need to believe that He will use our background for our own good.

Two

E T ERNALIZE

Trust God

"For the word of the Lord is right and true; he is faithful in all

he does" (Psalm 33:4 NIV)

Jackson remembered the moment in his parents' lives that permanently changed the direction of his. After years of witnessing intense arguments and near physically violent behavior, he watched as his parents decided to separate. The arguments had become the norm. It was agreed upon that twelve-year-old Jackson would live with his dad, at least until his mother could get help with her emotional outbursts. They had become so increasingly violent that Jackson secretly preferred not to live with either parent. In fact, he found himself picking up an argumentative attitude and feeling angry.

His mother moved in with her sister's family. On Tuesday, Thursday and Saturday, Jackson spent time with his mother. Monday, Wednesday and Sunday were spent with his dad. His dad seemed to be at peace with the whole situation. He'd come home from work, fix dinner, and read until it was Jackson's bedtime. His mother, however, was fighting the change. She continued to be easily angered, sometimes at the smallest of issues. That was until she began to go to counseling.

Jackson said as he recalled this time in his life, "I had no idea what was going on. But it seemed like she was changing and life was getting calmer."

After six months of living between his mother's and father's residences, his mother returned home. Strangely, they quit arguing. Jackson reflected, "It was completely out of my control and there was little I could do about it. I had to trust my parents and believe that things would work out."

~ ~ ~

In a similar manner, Junior's mother, Michelle, learned to trust God through a difficult time in their young family's life.

On February 24, 1993, Michelle awoke around 5:00 a.m. to birth pains.

"I was a little nervous because I thought I was having contractions, but I had never done this before," Michelle explained. It was raining and despite the way she felt, she decided to attend school anyway. She had experienced back pains on and off throughout the day. She described the school day as one of intense labor pains shooting through her body. Nevertheless, she made it through the day and accompanied BB to his parents' home. Shortly thereafter, she began to time her contractions. They were getting closer at two to three minutes apart. The baby had announced a slightly early arrival. He wasn't due until the following week.

When Michelle could wait no longer, she finally told BB the news and watched his eyeballs nearly explode.

The couple had decided in advance that they wanted to have an intimate delivery, so she and BB attempted to sneak off to the hospital. So much for the secrecy, it didn't work. BB's family figured out that the two were headed to the hospital. So, BB was forced to explain to his family that he and Michelle planned to have the baby without the entire family crowded in a nearby room. Reluctantly, the family agreed to allow BB to call them immediately after Michelle had delivered the baby.

Michelle now remembers it as one of the most anxious times in BB's life. As they were driving to the hospital, BB could barely concentrate long enough to keep his eyes on the road. Every few seconds Michelle had to reassure him that they were going to make it. Not surprisingly, there was heavy construction on Interstate 820.

"It didn't help that his car was not the most reliable," Michelle admitted. They both remembered *puttin'* along, since BB's car did not accelerate to speeds over 50 miles per hour.

Finally, they arrived at Northeast Community Hospital around 10 o'clock in the evening. After being in labor all night, Michelle gave birth to Junior twelve hours later.

Michelle remembered looking at the nurse and saying, "Oh, my God, he's ugly!"

"Don't worry, sweetheart. He'll get prettier," the nurse reassured her.

As unprepared teenage parents, they had yet to choose a name for the newborn. So, when asked by the hospital staff what was to be the child's name, Michelle told them to put his father's name on the birth certificate. Hallelujah! Junior's birth had been a success.

Three years and six months later, Junior's little brother, Jalynn Michael, came into the world. He was only four months old when he was stricken with viral bronchitis. Michelle took him to the doctor. The physician sent him home and asked her to return if his condition worsened. Shortly after, on December 16, 1996, Michelle awoke to a quiet baby. He was normally fussy at night, but she knew how to settle her second son. On this particular morning, something was wrong. Jalynn had never fully slept through the night. She touched her son and noticed that his flesh was cold.

BB had just stepped into the shower when he heard a horrified cry for help. He frantically ran out, soaking wet. Michelle began screaming at him to call 9-1-1. By the time BB had the EMS on the phone, Michelle had already begun administering CPR. She was a medical assistant and knew what to do, but it was too late. Jalynn had succumbed to sudden infant death syndrome (SIDS).

"I remember standing up and watching Junior stare at me. He was three at the time," Michelle said. "That was hard."

Her three-year-old wasn't crying, only staring. He was likely wondering what his mother was doing to his little brother. One of the firemen who showed up to rescue Jalynn was a friend of the couple from high school. On the way to the hospital, he attempted to comfort Michelle by giving her hope, but she knew she had lost her baby.

When his parents returned home from the hospital, Junior asked, "Where is my brother?" Although the young family were not Christians, they defaulted to a typical response: "He's with the angels," Michelle said while wiping tears from her face. It sounded like a fitting response for a three-year-old.

Young Junior looked up into his mother's eyes. "Well, Mommy, just tell Angel to go get him and bring him back," he said. He was speaking of BB's Uncle Angel.

Jalynn's funeral was on a Wednesday. One of the local pastors, J.W. Matlock from Central Full Gospel, had come by and spoken to the couple about God. Pastor Matlock told them how He would ultimately be the only one to comfort them.

Despite her doubts and almost unbearable pain, Michelle decided to attend church that Sunday. Neither her mother or father attended church. They believed that a God existed but they chose not to live a Christian life.

However, in BB's family, his sister-in-law did attend. His brother's wife was a committed Christ-follower who went to church with her side of the family. That was the only connection to people of faith they knew at the time.

None of that mattered. With a sense of numb urgency, Michelle dressed herself and then young Junior.

"Where are you going?" BB asked.

"Well, I'm gonna go to church," Michelle responded. "If you want to go with us, you can. All I know is that if I died tomorrow, I want to know I'll be able to see my son again!"

Without uttering one word, BB turned around, went into the bedroom, and returned fully dressed.

The couple attended the church for a year before BB responded to the sermons. One Sunday, he decided to give his life to Christ. He recalled that Sunday when an altar call was given.

Someone near him tapped him on the shoulder and asked, "Do you have everything that you need?"

BB had thought the person was speaking in the physical sense and responded with, "Yes, I do."

Again, the person asked, "Do you have everything that you need?"

Given a moment to be honest with God and himself, this time, BB humbly said, "No." That was the first day he trusted God with his life.

He recalled arriving home from work filled with joy every day. Something was different about him, and everyone knew it. He tells the story of a church member standing up to share an observation of him. BB remembered the member saying, "I saw brother BB driving to work, and he was singing. It just made me very happy. I'm not sure what he was singing, but I'm sure it was about the Lord."

BB admitted, "I didn't know a whole lot about God other than the little that had sunk in throughout that year that we had been going to church. I was not trying to let anything sink in—I was just trying to be there for my wife. But God had different plans."

Shortly after BB made up his mind to trust God, Michelle followed. Michelle led the family to the church building, and BB led them into a relationship with Christ. Neither have looked back since. It came at just the right time, too. A week before Jalynn's death, Michelle was frustrated with living with BB's parents and fed up with the challenges of being a young wife. She had intended to take the kids and leave BB to himself.

Someone once asked Michelle if she would trade the family coming to Christ to have her son back. Without hesitation, she replied, "No, I know I'll see my son one day, but had not Jalynn passed, I'm not sure if any of us would be serving God."

Soon after BB and Michelle demonstrated their trust in God, BB's aunt began attending services with them. Next, his brothers began going. Today, all of BB's brothers and sisters are Christians.

And just like that, Junior's parents made a decision that changed the direction of the life of their young family. God uses our trust in him to impact our walk with Christ and our relationships with others.

Out of the horrible tragedy of Jalynn passing from SIDS, BB and Michelle Garcia placed their trust in God. Michelle knew that she had to trust someone with the soul of her deceased son. Why not the God of the universe? In return, they found new life for themselves and their family.

Michelle's response to the death of her son is important to note. She didn't respond in bitterness or anger. To some, it seemed crazy that she would take a step toward putting their lives in the hand of the God who had allowed their son to be taken away from them. Had she responded differently, would it have led to her family developing a relationship with God?

For the first time in their lives, the Garcias had clear direction and BB knew it. As he said, "I was just trying to be there for my wife. But God had different plans." Once BB was able to overcome his habit of self-trust, he could get out the way and let God lead their lives. There is a freedom that immediately comes with turning all areas of our lives over to God. Although no one could take the place of Jaylynn, the couple would go on to have two other children. Michelle gave birth to a girl named Reagan and later a boy named Jeremiah.

Trust is a fragile thing. It is easily broken when we or someone else fails to live up to expectations. Think about this. Many of us live in a way that shows we trust our careers, the people in our lives, our government institutions, and the people who represent us. We face constant disappointment. But our trust is well placed when it is in God.

I used to hear older folks say, "God can always be trusted." We find this to be true in the darkest moments of our lives, but why wait for that time to happen when we can trust Him now?

Three

ET**E**RNALIZE

Engage your era

"Before I formed you in the womb I knew you, before you were born I set you apart; I appointed you as a prophet to the nations." (Jeremiah 1:5 NIV)

~~~~~~

~~~~~~~~~~

Thirteen-year-old Brevon was the biggest sci-fi movie fan and critic in her family. She adopted this passion from her dad. There were familiar plot twists that she absolutely loved and anticipated would happen while watching these movies.

One familiar scene was when the hero attempted to escape an enemy by entering a gate, seconds before it closed. It was often part of what was known as the escape sequence. Brevon explained, "I've watched this scene so many times that I timed the characters and made a mental note as to what position the gate was in. Then I considered the distance of the character. I looked to see if the timing matched. If the gate was at the same position that it was five seconds ago, the scene was flawed."

Early in the school year, Brevon heard about a new, after-school movie club that was recruiting students. The flyer described the club as being open to most genres and all students. Brevon could hardly wait to join. When Friday afternoon finally arrived, she hurried to Room 151. Upon walking in, she noticed that she was in a classroom filled with boys. The only other female was Ms. Drew, who sat at the rear of the class, grading papers. When the time for introductions came, students were asked to give their name as well as the genre they wanted to represent. As Brevon stood up, one boy mumbled under his breath, "We're not here to talk chick flicks."

Brevon proudly announced, "That's good because I'm here to talk sci-fi."

The other boys laughed at the mumbler. Brevon confidently knew what she represented. Now it was time to use her passion to engage the other club members and contribute to the discussion.

~ ~ ~

Like Brevon, Junior Garcia knew who he represented. But first, he had to take a stance.

The month of August in the state of Texas was no time to consider cool weather. It was a virtual outdoor steam room. In North Texas, the average high temperature in late summer was around 99 degrees. As Michelle and ten-year-old Junior Garcia rode to football practice, there was the usual silence in the air. Junior had always been a quiet kid. There was usually little conversation between he and his mother, but neither of them minded it.

Still, on this day Michelle glanced over her shoulder. "You doing all right, Bubba?" she asked.

"Yup!" he responded.

Again, this was normal for Junior. He was simply a child of few words.

Michelle and Junior reached the Fort Worth Youth Field, and she placed the car in the park position. As Michelle stepped out of the car, she noticed Junior didn't motion to get out of the vehicle. He just sat there with his head hanging down.

Wondering what was wrong with her son, she asked, "What are you doing? Are you not getting out?" She waited for a response. With an assuring smile, Michelle momentarily locked gazes with Junior.

In a steady voice, Junior answered, "I don't want to go to practice."

"Okay, you don't want to go, but you have to, so let's go."

For the second time, a little louder and bolder, Junior said, "I don't want to go."

This time Michelle's tone changed. In a voice only a mother can deliver, she remained gentle but firm. Michelle decided to do a little parental investigation by asking, "Do you not feel good?"

Shaking his head, Junior responded sharply, "No, I feel fine."

Michelle's patience ran out. "Then you need to get out of the car and go to practice!" she demanded.

Junior did not budge.

By this time, Michelle was at a complete loss. Junior had always obeyed without a struggle. Something was seriously wrong.

After a moment of silence, Junior began to sob. Alarmed, Michelle asked, "Why are you crying?" Before Junior could answer, Michelle took a motherly defensive stance. "Did the coaches do something to you? Were they mean to you? Did one of the coaches yell at you?"

By now, Junior had stepped out of the car was leaning against the front passenger door, sweating and crying. Michelle paused for a moment to ask Junior to remove his gear.

After listening to his mother go through several other bad scenarios in rapid fashion, Junior replied, "I don't feel like I should be out there at practice."

Michelle laughed. "Why, you're their best player!"

Ten minutes had passed since Junior and Michelle had pulled in for practice. The coaches and several teammates were looking in their direction. Practice had already begun. There was little doubt that the coaches were wondering what was taking so dog-gone long.

"I don't really think I need to be on the field," Junior argued. He raised his head and said, "Because, I'm not doing enough for God, Mom. If I could be playing football for two hours a day, I need to be doing something for God." Although it was difficult to put in words his desire to build a stronger relationship with God, within that moment, Junior certainly tried.

Michelle attempted to reason with herself. She now recalls, "At that time, I was literally speechless. I didn't know what to say to him."

So Michelle just stared back at him and responded with, "Okay."

Around this time, BB, who was also an assistant coach, came toward Michelle and Junior. Motioning to Michelle and Junior with a wave, he asked, "Whatcha doing?"

Michelle looked into BB's direction from a distance, and shook her head, signaling that she had it under control. Once she returned her gaze to Junior, she asked, "Are you sure?"

"I just can't, Mom," Junior responded.

Michelle began walking down the hill towards BB until she stood within inches in front of him. She explained to her husband that their quiet but obedient ten-year-old was taking a stance. BB, too, became speechless as he quickly realized that they had transferred their faith to Junior earlier than they thought. The kid was still in elementary school.

While BB collected his thoughts, Michelle decided to be the one to explain to the coaches the reason behind Junior's refusal to practice.

Coach Brian had been Junior's football mentor ever since Junior had picked up a football to play organized ball. But make no mistake about it, this was football in Texas. This game is taken very seriously. Michelle cautiously began to explain. "Hey, Brian," she said. "He said he can't come to practice today."

Coach quickly laughed as if Michelle had told a joke.

"No, really, he's up there crying so hard he could hardly talk to me," Michelle said.

"Why, what's wrong with him? Is he sick?" Coach asked.

"No, he said he can't come out here and play today because he's not doing enough for God."

Coach Brian, with a straight face, replied to Michelle, "Wow, I can't argue with that! There's nothing I can say to that. Just tell the boy I'll see him tomorrow at practice."

Michelle remembered walking back up the hill to their car. Junior's face was red, and his eyes were swollen from crying.

This was Junior's first time standing up for his faith. She paused for a moment and relayed Coach Brian's response.

Later, Junior learned that he could represent God and engage his peers in whichever activity in which he participated. That included football.

Junior's silent demeanor sometimes placed him at a disadvantage for those who coached and taught him. On one occasion during the high school football season, his teammates supported him as a choice for a possible team captain. His coaches, however, disagreed with this idea. Junior's lack of vocal leadership was less than appealing for them. But Junior was not at all interested in impressing his coaches at the expense of being someone he was not. Instead, he led in the way he felt led by God: he prayed.

Michelle remembered the first time she witnessed this team engagement.

The game began as it usually did, with the team running through the tunnel onto the sideline. The team hurried through so that the game could begin. But while the most of his teammates ran and stopped at the sidelines, Junior, along with a couple of other players, kept walking ahead to the end zone. Onlookers were staring and wondering where they were going.

Michelle remembers her first reaction. "I was watching him and thinking, 'What is he doing?'"

After reaching the end zone, Junior knelt on one knee to pray for the team.

One game later, the numbers had grown and many on the team joined him in the end zone for prayer. From that time on, the numbers kept growing and most of the team ran through the tunnel, huddled up, and prayed before each game.

~ ~ ~

Have you ever wondered why you are alive in this decade, this century, this era? Whether or not you are a follower of Christ, you and I have a window of time. Only God knows how much time that window will remain open. We're not going to be around on earth forever. If you are reading this right now, it is not by accident. God has placed us in this space of time for a reason.

Early in his Christian walk, Junior responded to the call to represent Christ. As a ten-year-old, he sensed that there was more to his Christian identity than simply being called a Christian; he needed to *live* like one. As he said, "If I could be playing football for two hours a day, I need to be doing something for God." His spiritual alarm had begun to ring. At first, he may not have understood that he could take his faith with him everywhere, he realized that Christianity involved action and engagement. He wasn't exactly sure how that was to happen, but he knew it involved God and people.

I don't know many ten-year-olds who would have taken that type of stance. But Junior would tell you that he was no one particularly special. He didn't have any unique gifts or talent. He simply responded to what he understood at the time to be a commitment to God.

Nine years later he would approach his 1300-mile journey with the same mindset.

Junior also realized that he didn't have to wait until he was older to be a spiritual leader. He knew that because he was alive, he could pray, and praying would allow him to lead by example. So, he went to work engaging his team in prayer. He risked looking weird, losing friends, becoming unpopular, and maybe even damaging his reputation amongst his teammates and coaches. None of these things happened to Junior.

But it could have, and it could happen to you. In an increasingly secularized society, there is a cost for outwardly expressing your faith in Christ. Junior might not have considered the cost at age ten, but it set in motion a pattern of behavior that demonstrated his desire to engage the culture, and God blessed his efforts.

Engaging your era for Christ requires courage and boldness, whether you are at home, school, work, church, in the neighborhood or, as in Junior's case, on the football field. At times, you will be completely out of your comfort zone. You'll quickly discover that you are on an adventure that is filled with unpredictable people, circumstances, and outcomes. Sometimes you'll ask God and yourself if you should really be doing it. In those moments, remember that God created you to engage the culture and represent him in this span of time.

Four

ete**R**nalize

Renew your mind

"Do not conform to the pattern of this world, but be transformed by the renewing of your mind. Then you will be able to test and approve what God's will is—his good, pleasing and perfect will." (Romans 12:2 NIV)

~~~~~~

~~~~~~~~~~

Kyle Botts, the youngest of three boys, was born on December 8, 2000. He couldn't remember life without cable Internet, HDTV, or superior video game graphics. By age six, he was a skilled gamer. On the weekdays, Kyle would often play with his mother or two older brothers. On the weekends, he'd play with his dad.

As Kyle grew older, his family's gaming dynamics changed. His older brothers had part-time jobs, and playing with Mom just wasn't as much fun anymore. So, Kyle chose to spend time playing online with his friends from school.

One evening after dinner and homework, his mother allowed him to get in an hour of gaming. With his two older brothers in their late teens, she now had time to work at night while Kyle's father worked during the day. This evening, she was off from work and wanted to rest. She decided to take comfort on the family sectional while watching Kyle play his favorite action-adventure video game. It wasn't long before Kyle and his mother were playing.

Years had gone by without Mrs. Botts picking up a game controller. She was horrible. While the mother and son laughed at her awful gameplay, Kyle tried to explain the buttons on his latest controller.

"Give me some time, Kyle. It's been awhile, and I'm playing based on the old way we used to play," Mrs. Botts said.

Kyle paused the game for a moment and sarcastically replied, "Well, Mom, sometimes we have to learn a new way of doing things."

He remembered his mother's exact words while helping him with a math homework problem. Months ago, he complained to her about the different method his new teacher had taught the class. Mr. Bright told the class that he was simply teaching them to think differently about the problem. Mrs. Botts had countered Kyle's homework complaint on that evening and assured him that it was a better way of solving the problem.

This evening, Kyle knew that his mom had to think differently about the game because they both had changed since last playing. The game hadn't changed, but her thinking about the game had to change if she were to play well.

~ ~ ~

Likewise, involvement with sports helped pave the way for Junior Garcia to develop a different approach to the game of life. The approach began in his mind.

50

The athletic streak in the Garcia family ran deep. In addition to football, Junior also played as a point guard in basketball. His father, BB, often had various work commitments during Junior's high school years, but he recalled one coaching opportunity that allowed him to observe Junior.

During Junior's sixth-grade year, BB coached his basketball team. Both father and son were filled with excitement and optimism about the upcoming season, but when it was time to choose the players, disappointment quickly set in.

Basketball is played with five players from each team on the court at one time. Most teams have reserve players so that the starters can recoup their energy before returning to play. However, BB and Junior's team had only one extra player.

BB states, "We had six players. The other teams had eight to ten."

The team was made up of Junior, his twin cousins, two kids whose parents were assistant coaches, and a student whom the other teams had passed on. Some would have perceived this as a setback, and with good reason. If more than one player were to become overwhelmed with exhaustion or if a single player was injured, the chances of winning became significantly slim.

It would have been easy to feel defeated. Instead, the team worked hard, followed their coaches' directions, played respectfully, and executed well—despite having two fewer players than most of their competitors. The students on BB's team would not allow being understaffed to prevent them from working toward their goal of winning each game.

The opposing teams probably looked at BB and Junior's team, saw their number of players, and underestimated their potential. But BB and Junior weren't at all concerned with what the other teams thought about them. They knew what they thought about themselves was far more important.

Let's fast forward to one of the first games of Junior's senior year in high school. This time, fortunately, they had more than six players on the team.

It was Junior's team's first possession of the game. Junior was a point guard and he was filled with optimism about the upcoming season. The opposing team passed the ball with intensity near Junior's body. Matching his competitor's energy, Junior seized the opportunity and quickly stole the ball. Running as fast as he could go, he scurried down the court. He had his eyes set on a wide-open lane that virtually called his name.

But the moment Junior leapt, just as he was lifting his hands for the layup, a member of the opposing team thumped Junior on the back. The push was made with such force that Junior's body passed the basket, and he hit his head. His body had twisted so that he was facing the crowd, and he had missed the padding. He violently hit the back of his head on the painted brick wall in front of him.

Later, Junior stated, "I remember that game because it was something I had to overcome."

Junior's younger sister Reagan, also recalled the event. "When his concussion actually happened, I remember my mom running down the stands and literally sliding onto the court," she said.

Junior was immediately knocked out and fell to the floor. Stunned and frightened, Michelle ran toward Junior and slid onto the court to see if he was okay. By the time she got to him, he had come to and asked, "Hey, Mom, did I make the basket?"

"No, you didn't," Michelle told him.

Later they would find out in the ER that the push had resulted in a concussion and a dislocated shoulder.

Despite Junior's personal injury, the team went on to win two games in the playoffs that year. It was the deepest a Lake Worth basketball team had gone into the playoffs in twenty years.

Junior had to sit out for a couple of games. I'm sure there were times when he wished he were in the game but had to coast the bleachers, show support for the team from courtside, and wait for his injury to heal. He may have failed to make the basket in the first game, but he succeeded in recovering and went on to help the team go farther than it had gone in two decades.

Through basketball, Junior learned to think differently about his setbacks and to reassure himself that he would complete the Journey. In sixth grade, he figured the number of players wasn't the only deciding factor in winning or losing a basketball game.

For Junior that meant, they were going to have to win with those six players. What mattered were the number of points. Instead of complaining about what the team didn't have in the beginning of the season, he never approached it as if it were a problem. He simply led the team by playing his hardest and following coaching directions.

Then, during his senior year in high school, Junior had every reason to terminate his participation in the season. The effects of a concussion have can lead to lasting and life-altering consequences. Junior knew, however, that it didn't have to mean the end of his season. Once the doctors cleared him for a return to the court, he jumped at the opportunity to rejoin his team.

~ ~ ~

As humans, we all face both similar and different challenges in life. Unfortunately, there is no way to replay the events in our lives. We can't just press the restart button when failures or setbacks occur. Sometimes we get knocked down by others, treated unfairly, or we appear to be outnumbered. There are other times when, because of poor choices, we find ourselves having to take a break from playing.

In these moments, we're forced to confront doubt and negative self-talk. The enemy rushes in at the chance to remind us that we're not good enough, we'll fail, and we shouldn't be doing it in the first place.

The way to fight back is to renew your mind with God's word. Renewing your mind involves knowing that despite any type of setback, God has been and still is equipping you with what you need to continue and complete your journey. We must be able to renew our minds daily and not just when things are tough. The best way to do this is to remind ourselves of who God says we are, what we have, and what He says we can do.

God says we are:

1. More than conquerors (Romans 8:37)

2. Friends of Jesus (John 15:15)

3. A new person in Christ (2 Corinthians 5:17)

God says we have:

1. Deliverance from eternal death (Ephesians 2:8–9)

2. Power, love and self-control (2 Timothy 1:7)

3. Purpose (Ephesians 2:10)

God says we can:

1. Overcome obstacles (Matthew 17:20)

2. Escape from temptation (1 Corinthians 10:13)

3. Love people (1 Corinthians 13:1–6)

Begin with learning at least one verse from each group and you'll be taking the first steps to renewing your mind.

Five

ETER**N**ALIZE

Notice *God's voice*

"Be still, and know that I am God! I will be honored by every nation. I will be honored throughout the world." (Proverbs 3:5–6 NIV)

~~~~~~

~~~~~~~~~~

Sara was a college sophomore at one of the state's highest ranked universities. It was the first Monday in January. Almost everyone in the class was going through some degree of winter break withdrawal. The students returned tired, anxious, and irritable, despite having been away from classes for three weeks. They'd been waiting all morning to find out whether Professor Trammel would extend the deadline for the latest class research paper. The professor told the class that he would be giving them special instructions following the announcement. Until then, the students needed to wait patiently.

Following a few seconds of suspense, Professor Trammel announced that the students would get another week to complete the assignment. The lecture hall erupted in frantic cheers and giddy side-conversations. Sara also contributed to the chatter. Everyone was waiting to hear the instructions, but it was simply too noisy. The professor raised his hand to signal that there should be quietness in the room. Sara decided to suspend her expressed relief, stop talking for a moment, and focus in on what the professor had to say. Now everyone could hear the instructions.

~ ~ ~

In the same way, before the Journey took place, Junior stopped what he was doing to hear what God was saying.

As an incoming freshman at the University of North Texas, Junior had just registered for his fall classes and was ready to go home. He had arranged for his parents to pick him up from school. It had been three days since he had been home, so he was eager to leave the campus. Junior was ready to return to his familiar environment. As he walked to meet his parents, he saw something that immediately caught his attention.

In the center of the campus courtyard, directly in front of Junior, was a young man on his knees. He was kneeling on a mat and appeared to be praying. The school's students, faculty, and staff members were walking around the man as if he was invisible. They seemed to be uninterested in the activity of the Islamic faith follower openly praying at school.

But not Junior. He was completely captivated. His sense of urgency to leave the college campus all but disappeared. It wasn't the man praying that captured Junior. It was the open display of his faith that resonated with Junior.

Junior explains, "It was a time-stood-still moment, where I literally just stopped walking and caring about what was going on around me."

Junior started to question his faithfulness to Christianity. He began to wonder about his true commitment to the God he served. It was as if he suddenly realized that he wasn't living out his faith—at least publicly. Through the years, he had somehow become one of those secret Christians. As someone who was often characterized as an introvert, it was difficult for him to be vocal or demonstrative.

Junior believed that God called him not to be ashamed of the gospel of Christ, but he didn't know how to cross the threshold of openness about his faith. He wanted to display the love of Christ in his everyday life. He wanted to see God work in his life the way he read about in scriptures. Again, he wanted to do and be more.

That night, he and his parents attended church. He didn't say anything about what he had seen that day. Privately though, Junior would continue to wrestle with the concept of openly displaying his faith. Was what he saw that day just a coincidence and had little meaning? Or was this a major step in the life of a freshman college student? Whichever it was, Junior could not shake what he had seen and felt. He could no longer ignore that he served a God who demonstrated love for the world through Jesus. Why had he waited so long to demonstrate his love for God by sharing Jesus?

This private struggle led Junior to begin to seek God more earnestly by praying and reading scriptures. Junior confessed, "Before that moment, I believed in God. . . believed I had a personal relationship with Jesus, but I wasn't practicing it and living it on a daily basis."

In the weeks following the experience at school, God began to stir up the desire within Junior to live wholeheartedly for Christ. God uses our undivided attention to move us forward in our faith.

Junior stopped long enough to notice God speaking to him through a situation, and he took the next step in his faith. We often hear people say, "God spoke to me." At one time in my life, I thought that meant an audible voice, and I'd never heard it. Did that mean that God did not really speak to people? Not quite. . .

God often speaks to us through situations, people, and through the scriptures. If it doesn't line up with the scriptures, you should question whether it was God speaking at all. This is one of the reasons why learning the scriptures is very important to a Christian. If you don't know what the Bible says, anyone can tell you they heard from God, and you won't have anything to measure it against. That's another subject for another time.

Let's refocus our attention on Junior's quest. Remember, he suspended his desire to get home and the noise surrounding him in order to focus on what he believed God was saying to him. Junior described that scene as "a time-stood-still moment." This was not a "Paul on the road to Damascus" moment. Junior didn't oppose Christianity. He was at the time and is now a Christian. He was also aware that we are in a relationship with God. In any relationship, there has to be communication. For a moment, he took notice that God was communicating with him. When he turned his attention toward God, he started to receive what he could only receive from God, and that was the wisdom to live unashamed of the gospel.

It was as if Junior was holding back something from God. He wasn't fully committed to his faith. He knew that there was more to the Christian life than simply going to church.

Church is an essential part of the Christian life, as it allows us to worship with other believers, learn more about our faith, and serve others. The problem lies in thinking that this is enough to grow and become more like Christ. Anyone can regularly attend church, but God wants us to become much more than church-goers. He wants His spirit to live in us every day and all day. After all, we carry His name. Being still long enough to hear Him allows us to focus long enough on what He has to say to us.

In Junior's case, tuning in to God for those few minutes would send his spiritual life into overdrive. It wasn't long after that day that he decided to embark upon the journey that would forever change his life and greatly bless others. He sought after

God's heart, and a whole new life became available to him. He did and still does face challenges, just as we all do. There are certainly different levels to giving God our full attention, through prayer, fasting and reading His word. In whatever He's leading us to do, we should pursue it with our whole heart. Quieting the noise around you and listening to what He has to say to you will keep you in step with His plans for your life.

Six

ETERN**A**LIZE

Ask God

*"Ask and it will be given to you; seek and you will find; knock
and the door will be opened to you. For everyone who asks
receives; the one who seeks finds; and to the one who knocks,
the door will be opened." (Matthew 7:7 NIV)*

At exactly 8:35 a.m., the first period bell rung at Piedmont High School. In Algebra I, freshman math teacher Ms. Stringer explained the day's warmup before allowing students to complete a worksheet. Answers provided by the students demonstrated their understanding of the previous day's lesson.

It also informed Ms. Stringer of where students struggled the most.

Julian and the rest of his classmates had ten minutes to finish the assignment. Once completed, they were instructed to turn in the assignment for on-the-spot grading. Ms. Stringer didn't play around. She used her class time wisely with few exceptions.

While Ms. Stringer gave instructions, Paige, who sat in the seat next to Julian, whispered that she couldn't wait for the weekend to arrive. Ms. Stringer gave both students a stern look, but kept speaking. For the warmups, Ms. Stringer usually had students complete half of the ten equations. Then they went back and completed the other half together as a whole class. Since Julian was distracted by Paige during instructions, he didn't hear which half the class was supposed to do. He decided to take a risk and complete the even number of problems. After all, he didn't feel like hearing a mini lecture about the importance of listening to the teacher during instruction.

Julian completed the equations in half the allotted time. He approached Ms. Stringer's desk and motioned to hand her his worksheet. Without barely a glance, she nodded. "I assigned the odd numbered equations," she said. "Please return to your seat to complete the assignment. You have four minutes remaining."

Julian returned to his seat muttering to himself, "I should've asked."

A minute after Julian sat down, Paige completed her problems and had them checked by the teacher. Three of her five answers were wrong. She didn't understand what she was doing. Both Paige and Julian failed because they didn't ask for help.

~ ~ ~

Unlike Julian and Paige, Junior discovered that asking for help made all the difference on his journey.

Michelle and Junior were driving down Texas Interstate 820 in Michelle's khaki metallic 2008 Dodge Caliber. They were on their way to the mall to do a little shopping. Junior had just completed his freshman year of college, and today, although he felt hesitant, he had something to tell Michelle.

Of his parents, Junior had the closest bond with his mother. According to Junior, she had always supported him in every goal he set for himself. This endeavor, however was different. It involved a tremendous amount of sacrifice and danger—and some risk involving his reputation as well as that of their family.

During this time, Junior found himself escaping from the prison of public opinion. It must have been ingrained into him while growing up, but he realized that he cared too much about what people thought of him. To follow God wholeheartedly, he knew he had to break out. He certainly didn't doubt God, but he did *doubt* the reactions he would receive from those closest to him.

Nervously, Junior revealed his plan to Michelle: He believed God wanted him to carry a cross across the country.

He wondered, "What if she doesn't support me, and what if she doesn't believe in what I'm trying to do?" He also

70

remembers the courage he had to muster up before he said, "Hey, I want to carry the cross."

In the weeks and months leading up to this moment, Junior had been praying for God to do more through him. When he received his answer, he asked for courage and boldness to carry out God's answer. There is an often-used Christian metaphor that says, "We're God's hands and feet." If so, Junior was ready to walk with his feet and carry the cross with his hands.

Junior explained to Michelle that, in carrying the cross, he had a twofold purpose. First, he wanted to bring attention to the cross. In doing so, he would proclaim that Jesus is the only way to God. Secondly, he wanted to raise money to donate to Christian missions.

Let's back up for a moment. When Michelle, heard Junior say that he believed God had instructions for him, she paused. Her pause reminds me of the day on the football field, in his fifth-grade year, when she listened while Junior expressed his desire to do more for God. Nearly eight years later, that same desire existed.

Michelle listened, and then she gently asked, "Why do you think this is something God wants you to do?"

Junior responded, "I feel like I haven't been doing enough for him." Michele had heard this before.

Junior knew that he couldn't work his way into heaven. He was simply explaining that there was more that he could do to point people in the direction of Jesus, and he needed help doing it.

Michelle agreed but gave her son an uncertain look as she said, "You know there's gonna be people who think you're crazy for this, right?"

Junior shot back, "Yeah, I know, but what matters is what God thinks and what God has told me to do."

Junior had already spoken with Pastor Randy of the Oasis Church. He knew that sharing his plan with his parent's spiritual leader was of high importance. After speaking with his pastor and Michelle agreeing to provide Junior with their family's support, the next step was to address the church on Sunday.

The church service opened with worship in song and praise that Sunday morning, just like normal. Following worship, however, Pastor Randy began to prepare the congregation to hear Junior speak.

Everyone except Michelle, Pastor Randy and Junior were unaware of the plan and the reason behind it. Up until this moment, Junior had been his quiet and reserved self. Most of the church members had never heard him speak aloud, and here he was, speaking to the entire church at once.

Courtney, Pastor Randy's daughter, said, "Naturally, the room would go silent because of how little he spoke. So, you know when he spoke, he had something to say."

It was the first time that Junior had held a microphone in front of more than ten people. He accepted the introduction from his pastor and then began to share what he believed God had instructed him to do.

Pastor Randy said, "I think people were quite surprised and shocked that he even had a voice. Once he spoke, they realized, 'Okay, wow! He knows what he's doing. He knows why he's doing it!'"

In Mark 8:34, Jesus says, "Whoever wants to be my disciple must deny themselves and take up their cross and follow me." For Junior, it was both a literal and spiritual interpretation. While he was speaking to the church, Junior went further to explain how his complete surrendering to God moved him closer to his heavenly Father.

Meanwhile, his earthly father, like the rest of the congregation, stared back at Junior in shock. BB sat in their family's usual section with Michelle, and their other two children Reagan, and Jeremiah. He was overjoyed to know that his son was hearing from God.

BB described the moment. "I remember watching people and being amazed that they were showing this young man such respect."

BB was definitely a proud father, but he was also fascinated by the show of support from the church congregation.

~ ~ ~

Junior's prayer for God to use him opened doors that Junior never would have opened by himself. Notice that when he asked, it was not for selfish reasons. He didn't ask God to multiply his finances. He didn't ask for a car. While there is nothing wrong with asking God for material needs, God is certainly not a genie. Instead, Junior asked God to use him in any way that the Lord wanted to use him.

I believe this is a critical piece in terms of how we are to ask God. Before breaking out a laundry list of wants and needs, approach God with this mindset: "Lord, what do You want me to do?" When we approach God in this manner, we are acknowledging that His priorities, not our own, are first in our lives.

During Junior's initial declaration to Michelle, he pointed out, "I feel like I haven't been doing enough for Him." When

Junior asked God to use him, he realized that it was not for his own glory or praise. He's no different from the rest of us. We all spend too much time thinking about ourselves. But this was not one of those selfish prayers. This time, he got it right. Being used by God was all about *God* and not Junior.

Too often when we pray, it's as if we have a side agenda. It's as if we want God to work out our plans instead of us working out His plans.

Junior would never have had the support for the Journey from those around him, had he not asked. He didn't know whether his own parents would support him, but he asked. For example, during the conversation with his mother, the thought "What if she doesn't support me?" crossed his mind. He wasn't sure if his own mother would sign on to give up her summer vacation to back his journey. This is the woman who had supported him in every sporting event, school activity, and spiritual pursuit. Asking for support began with God but didn't stop there for Junior.

Junior first asked God what he could do for the kingdom, and then all heaven broke loose. God uses our "no strings attached" requests to demonstrate His power in our lives. As you might suspect, Junior was able to accomplish the Journey because of a simple request. Is it possible that all our communication with the Lord should contain the question, "Lord how would you like to use me?"

Whatever we need from God, including what His plans are for us, He encourages us to ask.

Seven

ETERNA**L**IZE

***Learn** adversity's purpose*

"Consider it pure joy, my brothers and sisters, whenever you face trials of many kinds, because you know that the testing of your faith produces perseverance. Let perseverance finish its work so that you may be mature and complete, not lacking anything." (James 1:2–4 NIV)

During the summer after her eleventh-grade year, Brianna's family moved away to a nearby state. Brianna's mother was a finance manager for a large corporation, and when the CEO asked her to transfer, she complied. It would be tough on the family, but her parents were confident that Brianna would adapt and quickly make new friends.

Brianna wasn't so sure. She had spent the past six years in the same school building. The school was divided into two sections. One part was for the middle school students, the other for the high school. It was a small school with only 700 students enrolled, but it was warm and friendly. There were a few unruly kids, but, overall, they respected each other.

The beginning of her senior year came quickly. Since she had completed twenty of the required twenty-two credits needed to graduate, Brianna decided to take a part-time job. She worked for a cookie kiosk at the local mall. Her shift usually ended at five o'clock in the afternoon. While walking to her 2010 Kia Soul parked out front, Brianna noticed a group of girls who stood near the entrance and exit doors of the east end of the mall.

"What the heck are you looking at?" one of the teens said in a snarly, sarcastic manner. She acted as if she knew Brianna.

"I'm just trying to go home," Brianna answered. The girls giggled as she walked by and left the building.

Brianna wasn't used to any type of confrontation from other students. She was friendly, attractive, and had a great personality. She began to wonder whether moving would damage her life.

The exact same verbal exchanged happened again at the end of the week. Brianna was confused as to what issue the girls had with her. This time, she stopped, walked closer to the group of girls, and said hello.

Immediately, there was a surprised expression on the face of the girl who had been taunting her. "Girl," she began, "All this time I thought you were someone else. I'm sorry. My name is Alondra."

The girls apologized and Brianna became acquainted with them. Brianna and Alondra have since become good friends.

~ ~ ~

Junior, too, would face adversity on the Journey that turned into a blessing.

The Journey team, which included Junior's family, church members and friends, had been permitted to remain on the interstate through Texas without any interference from law officials. They had spent a year planning for this trip. Before traveling through Arkansas, the team had called state officials in advance and received permission to walk there. By walking on the interstate, Junior's journey would be more visible to the public. The team had planned to walk along the interstate for the entire trip.

The group would progress through Texas and Arkansas. Organized and structured, they adhered to a daily routine. They would choose a starting point. Junior would begin walking, often with team members trailing behind him. The van would be driven to track mileage and provide support for the team.

Upon entry into Memphis, Tennessee, the Griffiths, a military family, had put the team up for the night in their home near Highway 51. The next morning, to avoid walking in the high traffic areas, the Journey team drove out to the east edge of the city to begin on I-40 for the day. Not long after they began for the day, the team was pulled over by a Tennessee state trooper. The trooper stepped out of his vehicle to politely tell Pastor Randy and the team that they would have to choose an alternate route. He was in no way disrespectful to Junior or the team. He simply felt that it would be too dangerous for the team to continue along the busy interstate. To confirm that he was making the right decision, the trooper phoned his superior. His superior agreed that the team would not be allowed to walk on I-40 in Tennessee.

BB had finished his work for the week and had left Texas to join the team in Tennessee. He recalled, "The trooper did not want to ask us to get off the highway, but they had a trooper recently get hit while on a stop."

Junior clearly remembered everyone appearing to be outwardly frustrated. "We'd already made it through two states with no major hiccups. Here we were in Tennessee, and the plans changed."

Pastor Randy suspected that it was more than the troopers simply doing their jobs. "I think this is more of you guys trying to shut down what God is doing. We're going to obey the law, but still get to our destination," he told one of the troopers.

The team packed up, loaded the van, and had a meeting. Immediately after the meeting, Pastor Randy called the Tennessee governor's office. He left a message without expecting a call back, but shortly thereafter he received a return call. It was the state's lieutenant governor.

The lieutenant governor explained to Pastor Randy that the number of recent deaths and accidents on the interstate were what prompted the restriction. In response to the traffic tragedies, they had begun to enforce the no pedestrian on major thoroughfares policy.

Pastor Randy reassured the Lieutenant Governor that the team would comply with the rules. However, he wanted it to be known that the alternate route, which was suggested by the state trooper, was more dangerous than their planned route. Parts of Route 70 ran parallel to I-40 and the road had no shoulder. Without a shoulder, in the event of a vehicle emergency or breakdown, there is nowhere to safely pull over. Roads without shoulders leave pedestrians vulnerable.

Still the governor's office wouldn't budge. So, it was settled: the Journey team would have to continue along Route 70. The team was there to honor God and to support each other even in this major setback.

Pastor Dan, who drove the van for the Journey, vividly remembered that day. He recalled, "When it didn't go according to plan, to me it wasn't a negative. It was like the Lord was saying, 'I let you do it your way up until now, but now let me show you how much better a plan I have.'"

The team decided to go to the nearest fuel station to purchase a road atlas and fuel up. Pastor Dan took their last $100 bill from the money pouch which was reserved for roadside donation to pay for the fuel and atlas. He told the clerk that the money might not fill up the van, but he intended to try.

"I'll hold your money here. Go ahead and fill up and we'll settle up afterwards," the clerk said.

After fueling the van, Pastor Dan returned to retrieve whatever change was left. The clerk returned a huge sixty-nine cents to Pastor Dan. He grabbed the change and receipt and headed toward the van. Once on board, he looked around, playfully pretended to cry and jokingly said, "This is all that's left of a $100 bill." He put the change in the team's change box, jumped in the driver's seat and began driving.

A few miles down the road, Junior said to Dan, "That looks like a good place for me to start." So, Dan pulled over, let him out and Junior began his cross-walk for the day. Shortly after Junior began walking, the driver of a car made a sudden stop and pulled over to get a bit closer. The woman had just taken her daughter to a dental appointment when she saw Junior, the cross, and his team. She quickly whipped out a $100 donation from her purse.

She wouldn't be the only one to provide support that day. As they arrived in town for the night, representatives from five churches in the area approached the team. They wanted to feed the team. Dan said, "It was like the whole town was fighting over who would put us up for the night, and feed us. We're talking about five different denominations."

By the end of the day, the five churches had pooled their resources and put on a dinner for the team. Everyone ate and held a prayer meeting for Junior and the team. The day began with the team spending their last $100, but ended up being the single biggest day for donations.

~ ~ ~

One of the ways God uses adversity is to develop our faith, which leads to strength of character. Junior and the team's faith was tested early during the Journey. Hypothetically, some might say that if everything would have gone as planned, the team may have quickly become prideful. When things seem to fall into place, we humans tend to want to take the credit. After all, we did all the work, right? *Wrong!* God enabled us to do it, and He should get the credit.

When reflecting on this part of the Journey, Junior admitted, "We'd already made it through two states without any major hiccups." But, although the team had traveled to Tennessee on their own plans, they were quickly reminded whose plans were more important. When rerouted, their level of dependence on God had to rise a notch. This was because the backroads would provide less visibility for the crew, and less visibility meant fewer donations. At least that's what they thought. Furthermore, they were running low on funds. But by the end of the day, the team ended up with five times as much in donations, new friends and supporters—and a hot meal.

Clearly God knows how to show us that his words are true. He will take care of us. We have to trust Him while He tests our faith. When we view adversity from God's perspective, we win.

No one wants to go through difficulty in their life, but this is especially true when what they are doing is being done to bring God glory. Somehow, we've developed the mindset that if it's done for God, we shouldn't have much trouble. That's simply not true. In fact, because our faith and the faith of others is at stake, we may face even more trouble.

As Junior and his team found out on the day they were forced to change their route, it's worth it. In the Christian life, adversity leads to stronger faith and strength of character.

Eight

ETERNAL**I**ZE

Inspire others

"In the same way, let your light shine before others, that they may see your good deeds and glorify your Father in heaven."

(Matthew 5:16 NIV)

~~~~~~

~~~~~~~~~~

Mrs. Piper was watching the five o'clock news when she saw something that grabbed her interest. It was a live news story about a ten-year-old boy who was raising funds for kids with cancer. He and his parents had sponsored a fair in which people could play carnival games while donating to the cause.

Mrs. Piper herself had won a battle with cancer at age 65 and had recently turned 80. Her husband had passed away ten years earlier, and she lived alone. It was around 5:15 p.m. in January on the east coast. It would be dark in an hour and Mrs. Piper did not usually leave the house after dark. There was something about this evening that was different. She debated with herself for a moment. "What could I do to help? I'm just an old woman," she said to herself. But, somehow, this notion of helplessness just didn't sit right with her.

So, she called her only son who lived fifteen minutes away on the east end of town. He picked her up and transported her to the fundraising location. After helping his mother exit the four-door sedan, he asked for the names and location of the fundraiser organizers. "You'll see a large blue tent with white stripes. I know it's getting dark, but you can't miss it," a friendly teenage girl responded.

When Mrs. Piper recognized the boy whom she had seen on television, she peered into his eyes and said, "I'm here to help."

She had been inspired.

~ ~ ~

At his peak, Junior averaged more than thirty-five miles per day on the Journey. Prior to this accomplishment, he averaged twenty-plus miles per day. This feat was often achieved on worn and heavily-blistered feet. It was, however, through his bubbled and fluid filled bottoms that he inspired his team members—one of whom was his own mother.

In this case, it wasn't what Junior did that inspired Michelle. It was what he didn't do. Despite the pain and suffering he endured along the Journey, Junior did not complain. Michelle remembers one evening during the Journey. Junior had taken a shower and was lying across the bed near his mother. "What are we going to do with your feet, Bubba?" Michelle asked

"I don't know Mom. I guess I'm just gonna have to walk on them," Junior responded.

Taking care of Junior's feet was one of Michelle's tasks on the Journey. She hated to do it, simply because she had to bear witness to her son's pain. The constant walking made it difficult for them to treat his feet. If he wanted to remain on schedule, there was little time for his feet to heal. The blisters had become so frequently filled that they were forced to use a needle to burst them. On one occasion, when pierced with a sterile needle, pressurized fluid from the blister made contact with the room's ceiling.

Fortunately, Michelle's sister-in-law had spoken with a marathon runner. He recommended a tactic that he used prior to running. He instructed Michelle to spray adhesive on the soles of Junior's feet. Next, she would need to apply a layer of corn starch and repeat the process until he had multiple layers of foot protection. The runner warned her that the tactic was frowned upon by some, but that it worked. Michelle knew that it sounded neither logical nor safe, but they were desperate. They had to try something. The "corn starch" strategy would enable Junior to keep walking until he completed the Journey.

"That was hard for Momma to do knowing that he was hurting that bad." However, Michelle went on to say, "Even at one point, I thought, 'He can't get up and go tomorrow,' and he did it every day!"

Sunday school teacher Rusty Rexford recalls Michelle attending to Junior's feet. "He's lying on the bed with his feet hanging off the bed. She's down on her knees, and she's cleaning his feet and doctoring his blisters. The next morning, when he gets up, she immediately gets up and she's back on her knees."

He went on to describe Michelle and Junior's routine of treating his blisters, which at times were a bit larger than a silver dollar. The thing that stood out in Rusty's mind was Junior's determination despite the suffering. He remembers that those who were concerned about Junior told him that he might have to reconsider his plan. At one point, Junior stated, "I don't care if they hurt or not, I still have to get up in the morning. I still have to get this done."

An inspired Rusty stated, "It was pretty amazing to see the determination there. Despite his feet hurting or injured, blistered or bleeding, he was still gonna make sure that he completed his walk." Rusty continued by saying that there are people of all ages who give up at the slightest bit of pain and discomfort or resistance. Junior, who could barely stand, refused to be defeated, and because of this, he accomplished his goal.

"It was a huge admirable characteristic," Rusty said. He was referring to the quality that he saw within Junior—determination.

~ ~ ~

God has placed personal characteristics in each Christian which encourages and motivates other people along the way.

Junior displayed an attitude of long-suffering and determination that inspired those around him. Early on the Journey he faced several obstacles, but walking on blistered feet was of a different type. He could have quit without anyone blaming him. After all, how could anyone expect him to walk to Washington, D.C. in aching discomfort? Although the physical soreness was his to bear alone, his mother would share the emotional sting of watching her son suffer. However, as she watched him endure the agony, something was stirred up inside of her. She realized that his selfless action was not for her to advise against. The Journey was bigger than Junior, her, the Garcia family or the entire team. Michelle understood that, as a mother, part of her job was to protect her children. But at this moment their mother needed simply to support her son. Junior was being used by God for the purpose of bringing God's kingdom glory. Her motherly role would have to change for Junior to complete the trip. What an impact this must have also had on sibling witnesses Regan and Jeremiah. As part of the Journey team, they experienced firsthand the spiritual power we have when following Christ.

Junior was unable to allow something as small as tortured feet to hold him back from being obedient to the God he served. His mindset was established from the beginning of the Journey."

Rusty had spent time with Junior as his church College and Career teacher. It was part of his job-description to try to inspire youth for Christ. He quickly realized that what he was witnessing was a turning of the tables, and he enjoyed it! Junior let his determined mindset and self-less qualities shine in such a way that even those closest to him were moved.

When we are uncompromising in our approach to serving the Lord, people become convinced that our relationship with Him is authentic. It's funny how that works. When we unselfishly display the characteristics that God has placed within us, people around us are inspired.

Nine

ETERNALI**Z**E

Zoom-in on the cross

"Then Jesus said to his disciples, 'Whoever wants to be my disciple must deny themselves and take up their cross and follow me.'" (Matthew 16:24)

~~~~~~

~~~~~~~~~~~

During Kailee's first soccer season, at least once a game she would stop, pluck a dandelion from the field, and run over to present it to her grandfather. He faithfully sat near the sidelines. He'd thank the five-year old with a kiss and send her back onto the field.

Now, a high school senior, long gone were the days when Kailee would be so easily distracted. She averaged three goals a game with her astonishing speed, and she had been offered three athletic scholarships to play in college.

Tonight was the Class 5A championship game. It was a tough one. The score remained 1–1 for most of the game. Both teams had had opportunities, but they had been unable to convert since the first half. Kailee's team, Brownsville Catholic, struck first in the 11th minute, but they had gone cold ever since. With twenty seconds left on the clock, Kailee unloaded a right-footed blast and sent the ball zooming inside the far post for the winning score.

After the game, her proud grandpa asked her about the winning kick. "You were double-teamed the entire game. How did you make that last goal?"

Kailee replied, "Well, for the last few seconds, I tuned out everything around me and made the goal the most important thing on my mind."

~ ~ ~

Junior Garcia must have done the same as he neared completion of the Journey.

It was Day 37. The Journey had come to an end. With barely a mile left until Junior reached his destination of the White House, he stopped walking. Along with members of the Journey team, he made a quick decision. He asked the rest of the team to walk the remaining seven blocks to greet the gatherers of the prayer celebration. Junior decided to take his final steps with the two most important men in his life. The two men were his biological father, BB, and his spiritual father, Pastor Randy.

Several people who had arrived to meet Junior wanted to walk with him during those final steps. BB felt as if they should, mildly disagreeing with his son. In BB's opinion, their supporters had sacrificed greatly to be there. It had been a thirty-seven-day journey during the middle of summer—a large chunk of June and July. Friends and family had foregone their vacations, donated money, and taken time off work to be physically present in D.C. BB could not understand why these people, who gave so much, could not share in the elation of completing the Journey alongside his son.

In haste, BB decided to walk away with the crowd. But before he could completely turn around, Junior gazed into his eyes and said with authority, "No, I want you to come with me. You and pastor are two of the most influential men in my life."

BB admits that at first, he didn't understand his son's logic. "I felt like he was being selfish," BB said. But that thinking didn't last long. BB stated, "I knew I wasn't listening to God. I was listening to what people wanted. Junior was the one who was in tune with God." BB admits that his son, unlike himself, was not trying to please everyone. He continued, "Had everybody walked in at the same time, the focus would not have been on the cross, it would've been on the group."

At all points along the Journey, Pastor Randy had paid close attention to Junior's demeanor. He was there to support him, but he also acknowledged that he was the teen's spiritual and emotional leader. So, as best as he could, he monitored every change in attitude displayed by Junior. On this day, the pastor noticed something different from the other thirty-six days. The pastor described a bit of sadness in Junior's demeanor.

Pastor Randy explained, "When we were about to complete walking, it was as if there was another transformation in demeanor." Pastor Randy continued, "This is it. We're going to walk in with boldness." Junior's facial expression seemed to convey this attitude for the pastor.

The men slowly walked toward the White House. They took a left and then the black iron gates were in full view. When they finally arrived, there were nearly one hundred supporters wearing red "Journey" shirts lined up on both sides as if they were waiting to greet the players following a college football game. These supporters, however, were preparing to pray and thank God for what He had done through Junior.

Junior had walked 1,225 of the 1,367 miles he set out to accomplish. Consider the fact that there were severe road conditions that they had to get around at times. Being 142 miles short of the total estimated mileage did not disqualify them from the goal of reaching the White House with the gospel.

As the three walked into the park area, the focus was on Junior, who quickly gave all credit to what Christ had accomplished on the cross.

~ ~ ~

God uses our focus on the cross to give us a life that's greater than what we had planned for ourselves.

Junior's single-mindedness allowed him to direct attention to the cross and attempt to redirect any attention drawn to himself. The Bible reminds us to pick up our cross and follow Jesus. In the first century, the cross meant one thing: death. If you were told to carry the cross, that meant that you were going to die in one of the most demeaning and humiliating ways known to man at the time.

Then and now, we are asked to let our own loyalties, desires, habits, and concerns die in exchange for God's. In like manner, we're acknowledging that we can do nothing without our Savior.

As Junior adopted this attitude, he made God his priority. This mindset allowed Junior to make a lasting impact in the lives of those who witnessed the Journey. It also allowed him to help the people who were watching to focus on the significance of the cross. Junior knew that it was neither he nor the crowd who should be praised, only the One who had died on the cross.

Central to our faith as Christians, it was the cross that revealed the heart of God. It was the cross that demonstrated His unconditional love for us. God is holy and just and, even though He created us, He could not allow us to continue in sin without punishment. It was Jesus's death on the cross, His burial, and His resurrection that gave us the opportunity to be in a right relationship with a perfect God. For us, He took the punishment. Junior understood, at least in part, the power of the cross.

Thank goodness, we serve a God who knows more about us than we know about ourselves.

When we zoom-in on the cross, God uses our lives in ways that amaze us and the people around us, because it's done in His *greater* power and not our own.

Ten

ETERNALIZ**E**

Express thanks

"Whatever you do in word or deed, do all in the name of the Lord Jesus, giving thanks to God the Father through Him."

(Colossians 3:17)

~~~~~~

~~~~~~~~~~

Tyler was not accustomed to tossing and turning before falling asleep. Rarely had he ever experienced a "heavy mind" at bedtime. His mother worked from 8–12 at her first job and 3–11 at the second. She'd usually arrive home at around 11:30 p.m. They would briefly talk about his school day and then they would say goodnight to each other.

Tyler was an only child, and it was just he and his mother in the home. He'd always been known as the brains of the family and he wasn't afraid to use them. At times people tried to mock his intellect, but most of his fifteen years were spent knowing that he'd been given a gift.

It began in third grade when his reading teacher discovered that he had the fluency and comprehension level of a sixth grader. Soon after, he was tested to confirm the educator's suspicion. Before the next school year began, Tyler was given a talented and gifted label. Near the end of his freshman year in high school, he'd been accepted into a school that prepared other talented and gifted kids for higher learning. The big difference for him was that it was in the wealthy part of town. Tyler and his mother were of a different social class.

On the first day of school he was dramatically reminded of this fact. That evening after school, his mother asked him about his day. Tyler paused in silence to collect his thoughts, then he responded, "Well, Mom, the students didn't wear fancy clothes but they definitely drove expensive cars. I'd never seen so many Mercedes, BMW's, and Porches all in one parking lot. School looked like a luxury car show!"

Tyler's mother just smiled and said, "You'll do well there."

Those words of encouragement didn't make him sleep any easier. He was worried that, even though he changed schools, he'd remain an outcast. Suddenly, Tyler had an idea. He remembered his mother telling him to count his blessings and be thankful for what he had.

"Let's see," he said to himself. "I have a great mom, a home to live in, my own bedroom, a gifted mind. . ." and before long, a big snore. Being thankful had brought him peace enough to fall asleep.

~ ~ ~

It was time to express gratitude to God for the completion of the Journey. It was also a time of reflection for Junior and a time of unity for his supporters.

The arrival was not without conflict. For weeks, they had attempted to get a public gathering permit to assemble at the gates—which is mandatory to conduct organized activities inside President's Park. Finally, they had the permit in hand and had assembled where they were supposed to be. But then the National Park Service authorities told the group that, according to their permit, they could not assemble there and that they would have to relocate. Also, they could not stand the cross fully erect in front of the White House. It needed to be laid on its side or flat on the grass. Any objects that stood taller than the gates were not allowed.

After negotiations and the signing of a new permit, they were authorized to move to a grassy area near the originally intended site. Junior says, "It was kind of a mess at first. But in the end, we had worship service and prayer at the White House."

Junior realized that although he had finished this journey, it was only the beginning of what God had called him to do. During the prayer celebration in the park, he thanked God for what was accomplished and what God was doing in the country. He thanked God for the support he'd been given and for supplying him with the strength needed to complete the Journey. He also prayed for God to raise up a people of faith and guide the country's leaders.

Mindi Martin, an Oasis Church member, gave her take on the event. "How excited you are! Everyone's heart is pumping and you know amazing things are about to happen! That's what it was like. Your adrenaline was just pumping. It was something that seemed impossible, yet here it was happening!" she said, laughing and gratefully overjoyed.

Another church with a large group had joined the Journey community in praising and thanking God. With the wooden cross in the center of the now expanded group of believers, they all worshipped by giving thanks. People were kneeling on the ground, their hands held high, singing praises at the top of their lungs. Mindi remembered seeing people earnestly praying, asking for forgiveness, and displaying a unified attitude all in a spirit of thankfulness.

Sunday school teacher Rusty described the worship service as pure joy and relief. It was joy for the Journey supporters and relief for Junior, who had completed what he believed God called him to do. They team had prayed for mild weather beforehand, and it appeared that their prayers were answered. At 83 degrees by late morning, the park was filled with people. Onlookers asked to take pictures and worship with the group. The initial number of Journey supporters had suddenly doubled. Those who chose not to join the group heard prayer and people worshipping, and they witnessed Junior standing with the cross.

Rusty recalled, "You saw a sea of people. It didn't matter what color or what gender. We didn't know if they were Pentecostal or Baptist. All of them were excited to see the cross. It was overwhelming peace and joy we were feeling at that time."

According to Rusty, everything seemed to line up perfectly for that day. Everyone was thankful for what God had done through a nineteen-year-old kid, his family and a body of believing church members.

~ ~ ~

Giving thanks to God reminds us that every gift we've ever received in our lifetime is from Him.

Junior and the Journey members concluded the trip by giving thanks and praise to the One who made it all possible. I'm certain that at times Junior and his supporters questioned whether they should go on the Journey at all. For a teenager, the task had to seem impossible. Even seasoned adult Christians were filled with thanksgiving and praise when the team reached its destination. Mindi didn't hold back when she said, "It was something that seemed impossible, yet here it was happening!" She understood how unlikely it was for her to be present at the worship service. As with everyone there, she had a personal testimony of God doing amazing things in her own life. She was thankful.

Furthermore, Rusty had just been laid off from work. So-called "responsible" people might have asked why he wasn't back in Texas looking for a job. However, Rusty knew that God had made it possible for him to join the Journey team. He knew who he depended upon. He also knew that God would bless him with another job. This was a day to thank God for what He had already done for Rusty himself and for others.

Without God, Junior never would have been born to teen parents who questioned whether they should go through with the pregnancy. Without God, Michelle never would have been emotionally moved to visit the church in search of answers. Without God, Junior never would have had the courage to risk his and his family's reputation. Without God, the team would never have reached the destination of the White House.

Let me put it this way:

- He knows our **background** – Chapter 1

- He knows **trusting** in Him leads to greater power – Chapter 2

- He knows the **era** in which we live – Chapter 3

- He's given us the tools we need to **renew our minds** – Chapter 4

- He knows how to get us to respond to **His voice** - Chapter 5

- He knows what we need before we **ask** Him – Chapter 6

- He knows how to help us **learn to overcome adversity** - Chapter 7

- He knows the characteristics he's placed within us will **inspire** others – Chapter 8

- He knows what he's done through Jesus on **the cross** – Chapter 9

- He knows **expressed thanks** helps us to maintain the right perspective about God – Chapter 10

Yes! God is worthy of all praise, worship and expressed thanks that we can give Him. However long or short your life has been, look back for a moment to remember all that He has been giving to us our entire lives.

The Journey became a live demonstration of a loving God giving the tools needed and equipping us for service to Him. He did it for a quiet nineteen-year-old college student. He's done it for others and will do it for you.

Ask God in what way does He want you to impact lives for Him. When you discover what it is, don't waste any opportunities. Prayerfully go and filled with the power of the Holy Spirit, **ETERNALIZE** Christ for others! Remember God is with you as He was with Junior and the group of believers in *The Journey of Junior Garcia*.

Ultimately, *The Journey of Junior Garcia* was written to help us along our individual walk with Christ. However, if you have not accepted God's best through Jesus, it is not by coincidence that you are reading this. Now is the time to surrender your life to someone who can do more with it than you could ever imagine or dream.

Please join me as we pray together. Repeat after me.

Lord Jesus, I am a sinner. Instead of the gift of life I have been given, I really deserve death. Forgive me for my sins. Today, I choose NOT to die in sin, but instead choose to spend eternity with you. I am unable to save myself and will NOT enter heaven by just being a good person. I confess with my mouth and believe with my heart that you are the Son of the living God. I also believe you died on the cross for my sins, was buried and rose on the third day. Thank you for giving me new life in Jesus' name. Amen.

Welcome to the family of God!

www.ingramcontent.com/pod-product-compliance
Lightning Source LLC
Chambersburg PA
CBHW021132020426
42331CB00005B/729